My Little Book of Hope

My Little Book of Hope

STORIES AND INSPIRATION
BY ADHD TEENS FOR ADHD TEENS

Judy A. MacNamee
Educator and ADHD Coach

Proving
Press

Book Design & Production
Columbus Publishing Lab
www.ColumbusPublishingLab.com

Paperback ISBN 978-1-63337-107-1
E-book ISBN 978-1-63337-108-8

Printed in the United States of America
1 3 5 7 9 10 8 6 4 2.

In Memory Of:

My mother, Dorothea MacNamee (1917-1974)
and father, Stanley G. MacNamee (1917-2007),
who both journeyed on to a different world before they had
a chance to see my passion come to fruition. I know they are
watching over me every single day. My mother was the real
writer and artist in the family, and although this may not do
her work justice, I have to think she is proud as her spirit
continues to live inside of me.

Acknowledgments & Dedication

My gratitude goes out to so many! Thank you to all of the following people for their support:

- Clare Luffman, who was a key player in helping my business get off the ground.

- All the wonderful mentors at the ADD Coach Academy and all those who work every single day in this field to reach children and adults struggling with ADD/ADHD. David, your personal call back to me was the catalyst behind this journey. You are all my daily energy and a vital inspiration to me!

- Brad, my publisher, for his patience with ALL my questions, and for his great ideas!

- Family and friends for their patience, and their hand in helping build the foundation of my business, and who keep encouraging me with their supportive words. It helps me get up every morning!

- The inspirational parents, past and present, who trusted in me and put faith in me to work with their children.

- Parents of struggling teens everywhere—I applaud you for all you do each and every day!

- The most thanks, appreciation and admiration goes to YOU, my struggling teens. It is you who have embedded yourselves in my heart and in the hearts of others.

- A very special thanks to Keenan, Missy Hood, Amy, Jake, Andrea, and Tessa Jane for the strength and willingness to pour out your hearts for this project.

This book is because of you, for you, and I thank you for bringing hope to others.

How Did This Happen?

My motivation for writing this book is embedded in the hearts of struggling teens.

Writing a book has never been on my agenda for life. Oh, there were years where writing was part of my world, and I've often expressed myself through poetry and silly clichés, many of which you'll still find on my yearly family calendar. But I didn't write a book just to write a book. I created this because I was so inspired by my students, and they taught me something I felt impelled to share with you.

In 2004, as an intervention specialist at Grove City High School in Grove City, Ohio, I was working with many fabulous, exceptional students. My days were spent teaching content, writing IEPs (Individualized Education Programs), creating incentive programs, providing intervention services, and all other jobs required of a special needs teacher.

I loved my job and I loved my kids! They were witty, creative, funny, and brought me countless memories. Yet, I watched them struggle every day academically and socially. I saw their self-confidence torn apart by their peers. I witnessed their frustrations and pain completing tasks that seemed easy to others. I tried to protect them from the school bullies who waited, salivating in the hallways for the "catch of the day," but it was an uphill battle every day.

Due to many variables I left the public school classroom, but it was those challenging years, with those fabulous kids, that led me to establish my own ADHD coaching business. When you work side by side with these kids each and every day, knowing their struggles and their victories, you can't let go. They were, and still are, in my heart. By opening a coaching business, I found a way to continue my work with them outside of the school setting.

Yet, despite all those years of experience, all the conversations, all the battles and all the victories, one day I realized that I had missed the key piece—the one part of the puzzle that was blurred. The piece that was right in front of me for so long.

I knew that getting through each day was painful and tough for my students, but I never realized how <u>much</u> pain was hidden behind their eyes. Every day they faced the challenge of one emotion—difficult to see and difficult to express—the pain of being *different*.

Yes, my previous work helped me build my ADHD coaching business for teens just like you. This business gives me the pleasure of working with young adults almost every day, and I am able to apply years of experience and training as an educator and ADHD coach to make a difference in the lives of teens and their families. But...that key piece—that emotion, that *difference*—seems to come as a package deal with almost every teen client I work with.

It hit home with one particular student.

I will call this young man Alex. We had only been working together for a short time. One day, as his mom and I were discussing some school-related issues prior to my coaching meeting with Alex, he began expressing, quite negatively, his thoughts about school and his continued struggles.

I asked Alex, "How do you think you'll feel after we build skills to overcome these roadblocks and you move forward?"

Alex slumped down in his seat, and with a long exhale confessed, "I don't think I'll feel so different anymore. I feel so alone and don't want to feel different than anyone else. I don't like it."

I am not sure which hit me more: the impact from Alex's words, or the look on his mother's face. She had no idea that was how he felt. She knew he had friends at school, and to her he seemed to be a happy kid, but her face turned to stone when he confessed his loneliness and differences.

That was the game changer. Alex was the turning point in realizing that the feeling of being *different*—that feeling of being out of place and alone—was my catalyst for writing this book.

I couldn't bear to continue to see these young adults burdened with such a deep emotion. I wondered how many other teens like Alex there were in the world—those who not only felt this veil smothering them, but who never knew there was a way out. No, it's not easy, but that's why these young adults are sharing with you. They have been where you are now and they want you to know, you are not alone.

These fabulous survivors are my inspiration to continue to build on my work, but more importantly, it is because of each and every one of them that this book is being written and shared with you.

So, as you read the stories of your peers in this book, try not to focus on how each teen felt when they walked in my door. Instead, focus on the transformation they went through and how they felt when they walked out the door!

I want YOU to see that you are not alone! I want you to see yourself in their stories and realize that you are not broken, defeated or stupid. It's not a magic wand process, but a journey, and you can do it.

Feeling *different* is very personal. The many layers of "feeling different" can weigh heavily on your shoulders. My kids speak of frustration, feeling overwhelmed, fearful, hurt, anxious and shy. They say that they have a large knot that sits in their chest, crying out. Sound familiar?

Let's take that first step together. Grab hold of these inspiring young adults who have fought through similar challenges, and let them guide you into their hearts like they did for me.

When you arrive, you too may discover, like they did, that "being different rocks!"

It's time...

Time to shift the paradigm

Time to stop the labeling

Time to embrace diversity

Time to embrace strengths, not weaknesses

Time to CELEBRATE our students each and every day

CHAPTER 1

"The world will tell you who you are, until you tell the world."
—J.P. Moore

Feeling different? ADHD expresses and presents itself differently in all individuals. There is no cookie-cutter mold, and as a result, individuals often find themselves outside the box that society built.

The Great Big Book of Feelings by Mary Hoffman is a fabulous collection of children's books that help children better understand different feelings that we all struggle with in our lives. But feeling different to the point of believing you ARE different and an outcast in your world can weigh heavily on the emotions of both child and parent.

Christine Beharry, contributor to *Forbes Magazine*, explains different as:

"The odd one out. It's not easy being different. Being different means that you don't blend in completely with the status quo. It means that you don't perfectly fit into the everyday jigsaw of life. It means that what works for and applies to others does not always work for or apply to you.

"Sometimes, you may wake up in the morning and think that it may be better if it could all just stop—thinking that maybe you should be like everyone else, just to avoid the disparity and gain some sense of 'belonging.' But in times like this, just ask yourself—'Belonging to what?'

"Belonging to a mundane, close minded, innovative-less, limit-full existence where all of your edges and lines and aspirations can be neatly starched, ironed and folded and packed up into a box and placed on society's 'OK' shelf...is that really a perfect destiny?

"No. It's not. Maybe it's perfect for 99 percent of the people who surround you. But you're not a 99-percenter. **Embrace your differences.** What is good for the goose is not good for the gander. You have to determine who you are, and where you're headed. You have to determine what works for you... and what doesn't."

So, how does one with differences take that first step and embrace it when we have a society that stamps labels on differences and those who think differently? ADHD, for example, is labeled a disorder. If we look at the definition of disorder, it is defined as a state of confusion.

David Giwerc, founder and owner of The ADD Coach Academy, defines ADD/ADHD as a "unique brain wiring." How perfect! ADD'ers are some of the most creative and unique thinkers in the world! Where would we be without the unique brain wirings of our country's movers and shakers (Richard Branson), inventors (Thomas Edison, Alexander Graham Bell, the Wright brothers), creators (da Vinci, Van Gogh, Picasso), statesmen (Robert and John Kennedy, Lincoln, Napoleon), and athletes (Michael Phelps, Michael Jordan, Jason Kidd)?

Labeled a disorder, puts us outside the order. But, who defines that order and why must labeling help determine it?

There is another paradigm shift introduced that eliminates labels and introduces neurodiversity.

Neurodiversity involves a shift in our thinking. It teaches the focus to spotlight the strengths of people who think differently, rather than their weaknesses. According to psychiatrist and teacher Thomas Armstrong, "neurodiversity" replaces "disability" and introduces the concept that everyone on the planet has a different type of brain, just like each living plant and animal is different and contributes to the biodiversity of our planet. When we define our world this way, our education systems center on strengths and how to embrace and embellish them, not on categorizing people with labels of disorders and dysfunctions.

In the next chapters you will find six diverse and unique teens sharing their hearts with you about how they felt different, but more importantly, how they have come to embrace these differences. These are REAL kids, with REAL struggles just like you. The names have been changed but their stories are real. Some I know personally, but ALL are amazing individuals who have risen above their struggles. I know how difficult it was for them to write "their stories," but they found the courage to open up just for YOU.

CHAPTER 2

KEENAN

—be by myself

—hard to learn

—small annoying things

—don't like conversing

—it's hard to get through the day

—overwhelmed very easily

Normal people are normal, different people like me are different. I am not very good at talking; I like to keep things to myself. Every day is an adventure for me and my mom. I'm very particular about just about everything like: bright lights, loud noises and hot temperature. I am very specific about a lot of things like time and date.

When I went to public school it was very hard to learn because it was always too bright. I always got too distracted, and by the end of the day I was always so worn out and tired and I got so aggravated by the very small things. When talking or listening, I don't have very good eye contact.

From the Eyes of a Coach

What is behind Keenan's eyes?

More importantly, "WHO" is behind those eyes?

Keenan shares his heart so concisely about how the environment alone can be a struggle for his senses.

As you take another look at what Keenan wrote, consider these questions:

What small changes in the environment can Keenan make?

What could WE do in small ways to help him?

What's YOUR ideal environment for survival?

What could you do if you had the choice to change it?

"The most important thing in communication is hearing what isn't being said. The art of reading between the lines is a lifelong quest of the wise."

—Shannon L. Alder

CHAPTER 3

MISSY

This chapter is a special excerpt from Missy Hood about her struggle from age seventeen to adulthood. Learn more about Missy at her website: missyhood.wordpress.com — "Tame Your Braino"

My life has been "ANYTHING" but easy! ADHD wasn't diagnosed until seventeen years ago and I am forty-nine now, so the first twenty-five years of my life were CHAOTIC!

I used to drive by UT all the time wishing that I could learn like the other students and experience college life, but I knew if I attempted school the problems it would bring. Problems such as: massive fidgeting, the cloudiness that came over my thinking when I was under stress, which hindered my ability to concentrate, distractions and then failing out.

I attempted college three times before I finally completed my BA, and that alone took me six years. However, I KEPT TRYING! I recognized the patterns in the way that I learned with regard to my learning style versus the teacher's "teaching style."

During my jaunts in attempting school I broke into the film industry and successfully got a job as a theatrical costuming designer. I met a lot of famous people but I was still unfulfilled. I was unfulfilled because I knew that I was highly intelligent, and that even though most would envy my position, that position still wasn't my heart's passion.

I also lost forty jobs in fifteen of those years (I was a costuming designer in live production for seventeen years and in film for ten). I was forced to maintain dual careers so that I would always have income. The stress of it all was enough to make someone go crazy—let alone the way that I learned—and it wasn't until I learned about the triggers of ADHD (#1 trigger—STRESS—which none of us can get away from) that I finally had a pathway to overcoming.

I then took my newly found coping skills (which, at the time, I thought EVERYBODY knew about, but didn't) and promptly put them into place. It wouldn't be until I was in my master's program of college that I would learn not everybody understood the need for coping skills.

I have funny ticks and quirks when I'm under pressure (like sniffling all the time), which I now know to guard against so that I can pass it off like I have a cold or something. I still do struggle with relating because of the literalness in the way that I see my world, but I DO want you to know that I beat this thing called "ADHD." And so can you!

ADHD students beat the condition through applying healthy coping skills and through learning about their own weaknesses while maneuvering into cognitive maturity. I also want you students to know just how BRILLIANT YOU ARE! Did you know that you're a borderline, if not a FULL-FLEDGED GENIUS?!!!!!! I was told all my life that I was stupid because of the way that I learned. It wasn't until I had my IQ tested my master's year of college did I find out that my IQ is 162. That's pretty high, but my guess is that many of yours are just as high if not higher.

My book talks about my life, my ups/downs, my losses (some extreme) and then what I did when I decided to "get back up" and fight to WIN! This condition is beatable!

From the Eyes of a Coach

Missy's permission to include her story is so valuable, as is the message she has to share. Twenty-five years of chaos, from her teen years through adulthood, with so much struggle, disappointment and temporary failure, but she never, never, NEVER gave up.

Her self-awareness, development of coping skills and the way she embraces strategies that work *for her* helped her turn her life around and soar with success. But it was her tenacity, her ability to continue to pick herself up and try again no matter what the struggle, that is the real lesson in her personal story.

You ARE ALL BRILLIANT and can find this "FIGHT" in your heart, just like Missy!

As you think about Missy's story, consider these questions:
What do YOU know now to be true?
What are you tolerating that is not YOU?
What's holding you back from taking the first step?

"Our greatest weakness lies in giving up. The most certain way to succeed is to always try just one more time."

—Thomas Edison

CHAPTER 4

AMY

I overthink a lot. When I was in a regular private school I had to sit down and listen to stuff that made no sense to me for hours and I hated it. I was lucky and was diagnosed when I was little and I don't go to a private school anymore. I am homeschooled. When I do an assignment, for example a writing assignment, it's so hard for me to get it done because all these ideas about the paper are darting all over in my head, and I overthink and get really stressed out. I've always known that I think differently. I'm not a straight thinker, because one thought leads to another that leads to another and they may not be connected. Sometimes that's good for life situations, but normally it's a big problem.

When I was younger, I knew I thought differently from other kids and I still feel like that. I'm not noticeably different; I try very hard to make sure no one finds out. How I know I think differently is because I use different ways to get school work and other things done. Most of the time, I am shocked by how other people's ways of getting things done are so different. It's the total opposite of how I would do it. One of the things that I don't understand and other people do is reading. For most people, reading comes automatically. Not for me. I have to manually force myself to read, and even then it makes no sense. Luckily for me I've had people to help me get through this...my mom (who is my teacher), my ADHD coach and peers. The most important thing is to have self-confidence because it is so easy to slip into a depressive and low self-esteem state of mind.

From the Eyes of a Coach

Amy shares her story so well, sharing her thoughts and her observations: "Most of the time, I am shocked by how other people's ways of getting things done are so different. It's the total opposite of how I would do it."

As you consider what Amy is saying, think about these questions:

Would you continue to do it "your way" if you knew you could not fail?

Can you own the right way?

What did you discover about YOU?

"An essential aspect of creativity is not being afraid to fail."
—Edwin Land

CHAPTER 5

JAKE

For twenty-six years I have been living with undiagnosed ADHD. I was very disorganized and struggling at work, school, and life. I began to feel overwhelmed by what life had dealt me, and at times it seemed to drive my girlfriend crazy as well. I knew I wanted to become more; I just did not understand how I wanted to get where I wanted to go. I felt like I needed to know for sure if I did have ADHD. So I became officially diagnosed with ADHD and was prescribed Ritalin by my family doctor. When I took Ritalin something happened; I had increased focus, and a mild temper. I was so focused that my numbers at work increased quite a bit, and I was finally able to concentrate!

In the beginning, I was able to identify a key area in my life that I wanted to improve on. I wanted to improve my ability to deal with being distracted, or eliminate distractions if at all possible. An idea occurred to me! I could become more organized at home! So I then created a list of places I wanted to organize. It started in the office and found itself everywhere in the apartment. Over time, everything became way easier to find, and it became less cluttered and more organized. This increased my productivity at completing my school work.

Another key area that I am beginning to work on is losing weight, and also having more energy, and managing my anger through nutrition and fitness. I decided to hire a personal trainer to help me achieve these goals. In addition to losing weight, I've begun to keep better hygiene. It's improved so much that my dad and stepmom have complimented my image to my girlfriend.

I am beginning to take baby steps to the person that I want to become. If I had not taken that first step and reached out to others, I might still have been struggling and getting frustrated at life. I'm very excited about my progress and am looking forward to what's to come.

From the Eyes of a Coach

Jake had great success taking meds. This is a decision both your parents and you, as a teen, make each day. Jake was able to document how and what he did without them, and then document what changed while he was on them.

But whether you decide to go that route or not, what is the key? Reach out for that support and let others know what you hope to do. Have them help document the changes and stay with it long enough to weigh the good with the bad.

Jake did! Actually, several months later he contemplated going off of them, but he committed to seeing the changes and stuck with it long enough to know what he wanted.

As you ponder Jake's story, here are some questions that might help. There were many changes in Jake's life.

What are you doing to follow your joy and what does that happiness really look like to you?

How can you turn one wish into an action?

What's your role in change?

A little boy was having difficulty lifting a heavy stone. His father came along just then.

Noting the boy's failure, he asked, "Are you using all your strength?"

"Yes, I am," the little boy said impatiently.

"No, you are not," the father answered. "I am right here just waiting, and you haven't asked me to help you."

–Anonymous

CHAPTER 6

ANDREA

I am a very strong-minded person who really doesn't like feeling inferior to anyone. In a way this could be seen as a great motivational tool, but it was kind of hard to have motivation with my brain working against me. I'll get to that though. It also didn't help that a lot of my teachers told me that even though I spent hours on homework a night, and studied until I was blue in the face, I "didn't care" and needed to try harder. The worst part of this for me was that my brother was one of those kids who didn't have to try at all to get a 4.0 GPA (he graduated with a 4.3, just saying), and he's now getting paid to attend college, so that's cool I guess.

The actual worst thing was that I did care about school,

A LOT, but after a few report cards with far from perfect grades, and teachers telling me to step it up without giving me the step to step on, I acted like I didn't care. It made the disappointment I had in me, and from my parents and teachers, easier to live with. I eventually stopped doing all that work. I mean, why should I keep trying when I was giving 110% but everyone around me said I needed to muster up another 70?

My parents knew I wasn't doing well in school, but the fear of making me feel like I had to live up to my brother kept them from intervening. They agreed that I was at school for my social life and that I would eventually make it work. Although the only good thing about school was seeing my friends, I wasn't there for my social life. I was at school strictly to be shown how stupid I was for eight hours a day. I never showed my stupidity though. I gave myself a false sense of comfort by telling my friends I had grades just like theirs, that school was easy, and I got all my homework done in study hall because I was just that good.

By eighth grade the charade grew tiring and I decided to turn my life around and make my imaginary grades the real deal. I started doing homework with my friends so they could help me if I needed it. After watching how efficiently their work got done, I realized the hours that I spent studying could have been reduced to thirty minutes if I wasn't so good at distracting myself.

I had heard of ADHD before, a lot of my family members had it actually, but I didn't know it applied to me until I compared myself to my friends. I started asking them questions about how they studied and did homework. The one answer that still stands out to me the most came when I asked a really good friend of mine how many times she had to re-read questions, or passages out of a book. She told me she didn't have to re-read them at all. When she asked me how many times I re-read I said I didn't, but the truth was at least three to five times. It wasn't that I didn't understand, I just couldn't make it through all the words without getting bored or thinking about something else. I told my mom about this, and that I thought I had ADHD, but when she went to ask my teachers they told her that someone would've caught it by now and that I just wanted to make school easier on myself and that I needed to put in more effort instead of trying to take the easy way out. Jerks, right? So because I really was just a lazy kid who couldn't do well in middle school, I went right back to pretending I didn't care, when actually my unintelligent tendencies were tearing me apart inside.

I saw myself as a mistake; I mean, I had to be. How could

my parents have one kid who was perfect at everything he did, and then turn around and produce a mistake who couldn't pay attention long enough to read one paragraph from some book?

Feeling awful about myself lasted until sophomore year when one of my teachers, whose son also had ADHD, noticed the same symptoms in me. He told my parents and they decided to take me to the doctor and get this whole ordeal straightened out. When they said I did in fact have ADHD, a sense of I-told-you-so and relief flooded me. I finally wasn't this mistake that couldn't do anything right. I was just a kid who needed a little boost, and with that boost I'm able to be just like my friends—not quite my brother, but close enough. It just goes to show that even when something is pulling you down, if you can get the right help you'll be able to make it work and pull yourself up. I did.

From the Eyes of a Coach

"Although the only good thing about school was seeing my friends, I wasn't there for my social life. I was at school strictly to be shown how stupid I was for eight hours a day. I never showed my stupidity though. I gave myself a false sense of comfort by telling my friends I had grades just like theirs, that school was easy, and I got all my homework done in study hall because I was just that good."

What is your story?

Do you have a charade or story you tell yourself and others that may not be true?

Most people do, whether they are struggling or not. It's OK because it's part of our survival skills and part of human nature.

But, what happens if we continue to "tell our story"? You know...the one that really isn't true?

Andrea, thankfully, tired of the charade and decided to learn from it.

Do you have a charade? Is it really you?

"Facing the truth about ourselves is the hardest thing we could, but it had to be done if we want to be better people."
—Mary J. Blige

CHAPTER 7

TESSA JANE

It was a sunny day outside; however, I was stuck inside my house confused and frustrated. I was working on my homeschool science lesson by myself. The big words were getting jumbled in my head. I had this strong urge to do something other than the assignment. This urge happens frequently. I tried to defeat this urge by focusing more on the science, but it did not help. All it did was make things worse. I was in my daydreaming land, and I was thinking about the made-up characters that I think about often when I get bored. I finally made a compromise with myself to get up, dart to the other side of my living room, and then sit back down at my desk. This released some of my pent-up energy and allowed me to concentrate a little better.

I was then able to finish my science lesson. This is typical everyday life for me dealing with dyslexia and ADHD.

From day one of my educational journey I have struggled with focusing, concentrating, reading aloud, spelling, and paying attention during lessons. I daydream, think about five million things at one time, and feel like I have bottled up energy inside of me waiting to get out. The struggles are endless. I have felt defeated and overwhelmed.

I always take longer to accomplish any task and stay organized. My mind constantly wanders off into its own imaginary land, and I daydream about infinity and beyond! I have a vivid imagination, and I come up with very detailed scenarios for my characters in my head. I desire to be an author of a young adult fiction book someday, so hopefully this will help. In addition, I have been a poor speller. It has, at times, been humiliating to ask a friend how to spell things, because I feel stupid and embarrassed. I dread being called on to answer questions, because I am not very quick with verbalizing my thoughts. My thoughts are there, but I can't quickly put them into words. Once, I got in trouble during a class for moving too much and that really embarrassed me! I have even been told by someone sitting next to me to stop shaking my legs, but I honestly could not help it.

I have always felt that I have been different than other people.

A child psychologist tested me when I was in third grade. She diagnosed me with dyslexia and ADHD. This diagnosis has helped me to understand why I was struggling. However, I did not want anyone to know that I had been listed as having a learning disability. It made me feel weird and like I was the dumb one in the group. My father and mother have always told me, *"Tessa Jane, you have a learning difference, not a learning disability. All that pent-up energy will serve you well if you recognize it as a gift."* I think I am beginning to believe this now. I have gotten better at not feeling like I have to hide it from others. But, I still don't like the focus that gets put on me. At times, it still makes me feel like I am different from everyone else.

I have been fortunate through these struggles to have parents who support me. They both understand me, because they have similar struggles. I have also been able to meet other students who know how it feels. In fifth grade I made a friend who also has dyslexia, and this helped me to know that I am not the only one. The two of us would talk about how hard it is to read aloud, spell words, and do math problems. I was so happy to know I wasn't the only one with these difficulties. I then met someone else a couple of years later who has ADHD, and we quickly became friends. To know that I have friends who can relate to me makes me feel so much better.

I am in eighth grade now, and these struggles are still a part of my life, but are more manageable because of the efforts of my parents, intervention specialists, occupational therapists, and others. My parents have done numerous things through the years to help me. For instance, my mother has always schooled me at home by using an online public school curriculum, has enrolled me into a local co-op group, has enrolled me in a brain training program called P.A.C.E., and has taken me to many extracurricular activities. One of the most helpful things she enrolled me in was a college day event. While there, we met a coach who works with kids like me who are struggling. We were interested in how she has helped so many students that have struggled with ADHD. My mother scheduled eight appointments for me to meet with her. The sessions with her helped me tremendously! She is an amazing person and so much fun to talk to. She understands my constant battle with the ADHD and dyslexia. During our sessions, she helped me brainstorm ways to make my life easier. She helped me come up with ways to help me stay focused and on-task during my school work. I am so thankful I got the opportunity to work with her.

I have these struggles, but my parents, my coach, teachers, and many others have helped me to know that there is hope for my future. They have helped me to understand that I am not an oddball. I know God has great plans for my future! I am unique in my own special way. I wish for anyone who struggles with dyslexia and/or ADHD to know that they are not alone, and they have strengths like no one else. So remind yourself, like I do, that you are truly unique!

From the Eyes of a Coach

I find it fascinating but very, very meaningful, that every teen I have worked with not only feels different and alone, but often visits their "daydream fantasy world." Why wouldn't you? It's safe and it's there, and it's a place where you can showcase your strengths!

Here are some questions that may help you apply Tessa Jane's story to your life.

How can your differences be your gift?
How can we draw energy from our fantasy world?
Does what you do match up with who you are?

I know you may not all share this fantasy world with others, but know that so many teens your age have a similar place—away from stress, finger pointing and that feeling of hopelessness.

I do hope you can share YOUR world with others! I love listening to my teen clients share theirs and all the wonderful smiles and confidence it brings to them.

And I hope someday...this IS your real world!

"We don't create a fantasy world to escape reality. We create it to be able to stay."

—Lynda Barry

Conclusion

This isn't an ending but rather a beginning—*your* beginning, *your* stepping stone, *your* catalyst to know you CAN push those limits until they take you far away from the pain.

No, there is no magic formula. It takes guts, and it takes time, but like Keenan, Andrea, Missy, Jake, Amy, Tessa Jane, and so many more of your peers, they believe **YOU CAN.**

Embrace all you are and who you are. If you don't have a rich understanding of your strengths and who you are, look for help in uncovering them. Ask a parent or a mentor for five strengths they see in you. If you wish to begin that first step alone, find not just a few, but twenty-four character strengths that are YOU. www.viacharacter.org. If that first step is the hardest, we can help you!

I hope you can identify with the stories by your peers, and that they will truly make a difference in helping you take steps from the dark place, where you are now, to that new place of light and hope. From the stories shared, you can see that everyone's awareness and acceptance of ADHD wiring stems from a different lens. There is no normality but heralded differences.

Grab your inner strengths. Yes, they ARE there and they are many! These strengths are your gifts from all of us and your gifts to us. These character strengths set you apart from others— yes, making you different AND diverse—and these strengths make you the amazing person you are!

This isn't the end. Make this your beginning, one step at a time.

This is about you and your beliefs, your awareness, your mindfulness, your road to acceptance. I don't want you to be alone, so if you need a little help along any of your steps, please email me and tell me how I can help. I would love to hear from you! judy@adhdcoachconnect.com

WHERE DO WE GO FROM HERE?
CROSSING THE BRIDGE TO CHANGE

The stories presented here capture the struggles of six "labeled" teens who have overcome obstacles and crossed the bridge to change. They've been able to see past the labels, the environments, the structure of society and the archaic framework of our educational system. I believe there are and always will be some fabulous schools and fabulous educators out there, and I applaud you each and every day for your leadership and excellence. But, as a whole, our system continues to provide a generic environment for diversity to flourish. There are so many other struggles happening right in front of our eyes and I don't want you to miss them.

In Chapter 1, I introduced the term neurodiversity and its paradigm shift away from focusing on children's weaknesses and toward highlighting their strengths.

Thomas Armstrong, author of *Neurodiversity in the Classroom*, explains that the practical concept of neurodiversity replaces the use of the label *disability*, and introduces us to the process that

ALL of us contribute to brain diversity, just as each living plant and animal contributes to the biodiversity of our world. Hence, our education system centers on diverse students' strengths, providing environments that embrace and embellish them, not categorization and labels of disorders and dysfunctions.

Unlike the metaphoric comparisons of the brain to a computer that stemmed from literature in the 70s and 80s, more and more research is moving away from that metaphor.

Gerald Edelman (1987, 1998) explains, *"There is a degree of plasticity which allows it to recover from injury, and an ability to modify behavior through learning ... The brain is in no sense like any kind of instruction machine, like a computer. Each individual's brain is more like a unique rainforest, teeming with growth, decay, competition, diversity and selection."*

Imagine teachers treating each classroom as a unique rainforest, with brains of all shapes, sizes and wiring. If one were to have a piece of biodiversity, such as a flower or plant, the goal would be to nourish it so it would spread its leaves and petals in beauty. The environment would be altered specifically for that species, just as we do for violets, for evergreens and for our own gardens.

I have worked with many teenagers who come to me

struggling, not from their own brain diversity, but as a result of their environments and labels we've attached to them. These teens are beaten, defeated, suffering from guilt, low self-esteem, poor motivation, depression and anxiety.

Behind those walls of defeat is a beautiful child, corralled into his or her labeled pen and identified as ADHD, dyslexia, learning disabled, intellectual disabilities and more.

Imagine a world, a school, a classroom where individuals are nurtured to spread their creativity and become the individual they so long to be without shame, embarrassment or defeat.

It's time...

Time to shift the paradigm

Time to stop the labeling

Time to embrace diversity

Time to embrace strengths, not weaknesses

Time to CELEBRATE our students each and every day

www.ingramcontent.com/pod-product-compliance
Lightning Source LLC
Chambersburg PA
CBHW031634040426
42452CB00007B/822